§/13

100

Animals on Parade!

Masayuki Sebe

Kids Can Press

A band of **100** bears is leading a parade!

The Bear Band

I'm the bandleader.

Where is the bear wearing a rabbit hat?

Ack! A bee!

Are there really 100 bears?

More and more bears!
Count them: 32, 33, 34, 35 ...

Where is the bear so strong
he can carry a piano?

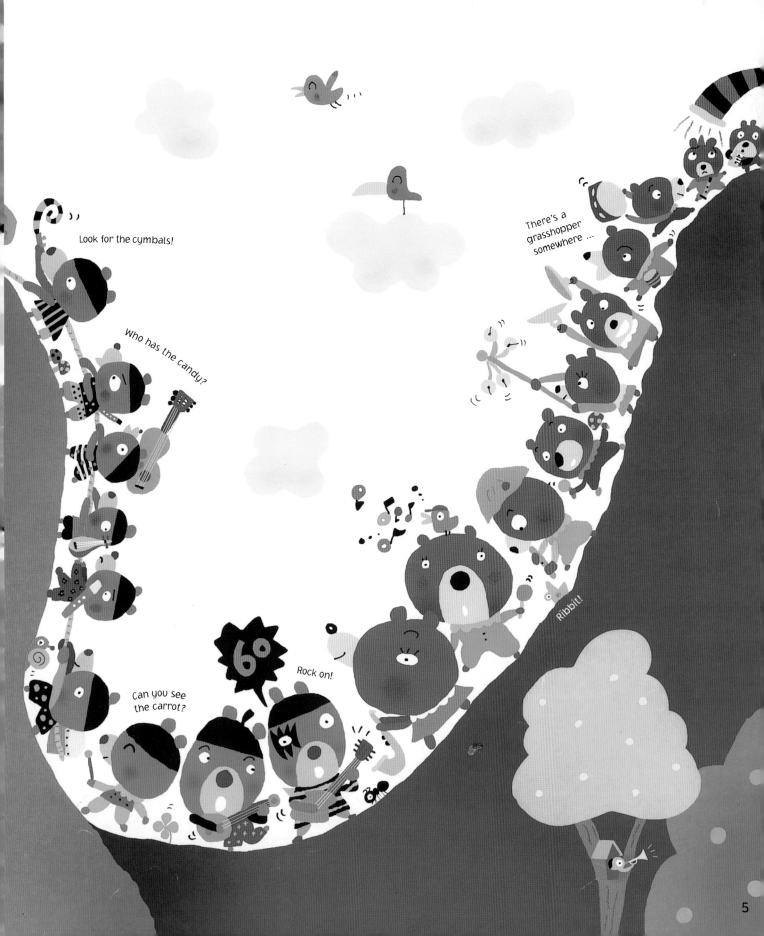

5

I'm number 71!

Where's the banana?

100 bear musicians.
Can you spot the last one?

Can you find
the fried egg?

There's a rabbit
here somewhere ...

Rise and
shine!

Now here come the pigs,
each with a yummy dish!

Can you find the pig
that loves carrots?

9

At last, pig number **100**!
What's in his pot?

Next come all 100 carpenter beetles!

Where's the baseball?

The Carpenter Beetles

I'm the first carpenter beetle.

Time to take off!

There's something hot in the pot!

I'm the last of 100 pigs.

Where are the biscuits?

The carpenter beetles are very strong. They're carrying lots of heavy things.

Where's the grasshopper?

Hurry up!

Where's the blue paint?

Do you see the butterfly?

Fiddlesticks!

13

Who's next? **100** rabbits in the Rabbit Circus!

I'm the last carpenter beetle.

The Rabbit Circus

Where's the apple?

I want a turn with the yo-yo!

I'm the first of the rabbits!

Circus rabbit number 13 has something on his head — what is it?

17

The last of **100** rabbits, finally!

Who comes next?

19

It's **100** birds on parade in the sky!

The Flower Birds

Tweet!
Tweet!

Chirp!

20

But where is everyone
going in such a hurry?

Piyo!
Piyo!

Faster!
Faster!

To the Animal Festival!

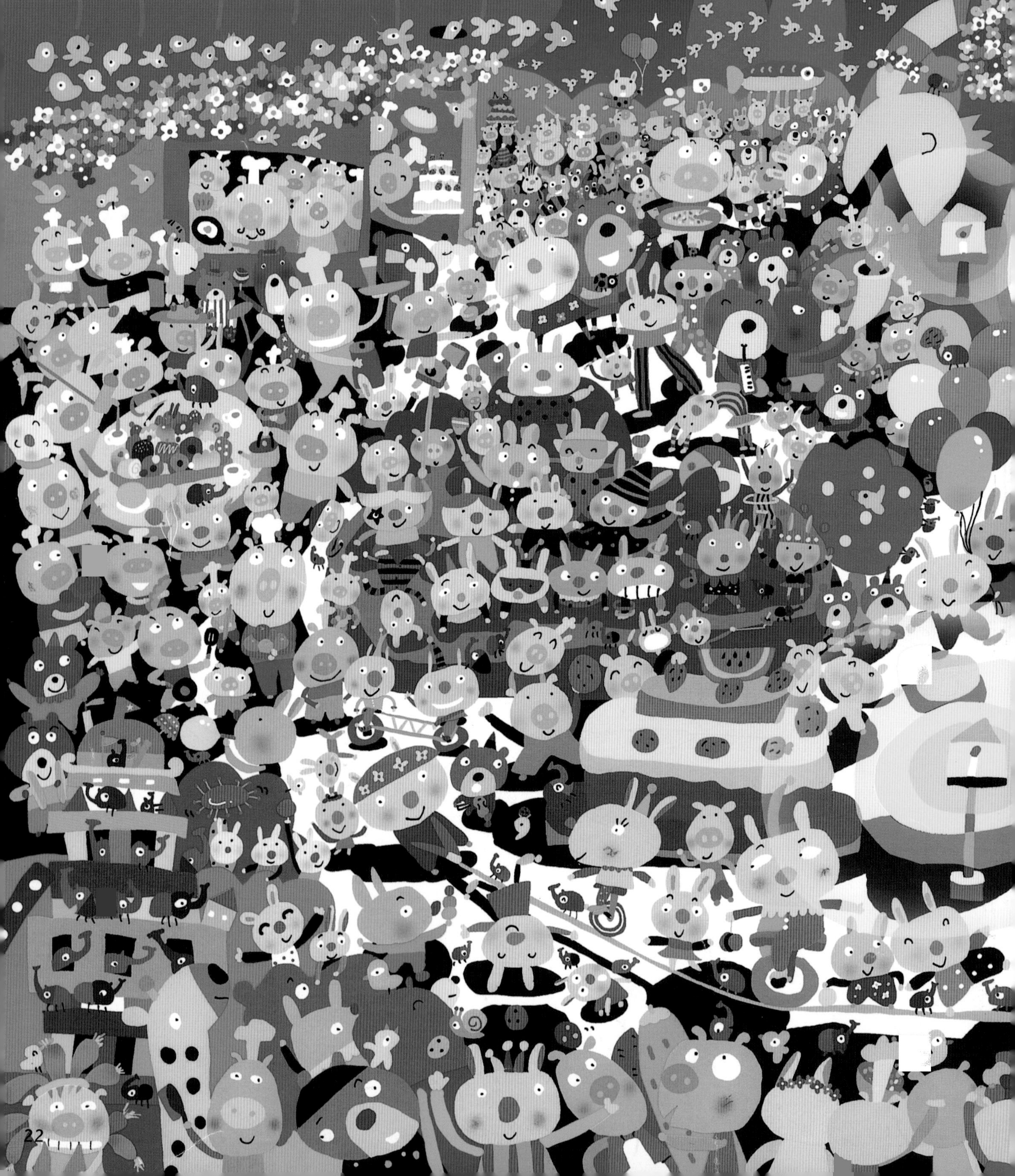

There's a snail, a ladybug and an ant
in every scene. Find them all!

Then look for these creatures and
things in the festival scene ...

Originally published in Japanese under the title *Dôbutsu Parade 100* by Kaisei-sha Publishing Co., Ltd.
English translation rights arranged through Japan Foreign-Rights Centre.

Text and illustrations © 2010 Masayuki Sebe
English translation © 2013 Kids Can Press

Kids Can Press acknowledges the financial support of the Government of Ontario, through the Ontario Media Development Corporation's Ontario Book Initiative; the Ontario Arts Council; the Canada Council for the Arts; and the Government of Canada, through the CBF, for our publishing activity.

Published in Canada by
Kids Can Press Ltd.
25 Dockside Drive
Toronto, ON M5A 0B5

Published in the U.S. by
Kids Can Press Ltd.
2250 Military Road
Tonawanda, NY 14150

www.kidscanpress.com

English edition edited by Yvette Ghione

This book is smyth sewn casebound.
Manufactured in Malaysia, in 10/2012 by Tien Wah Press (Pte) Ltd.

CM 13 0 9 8 7 6 5 4 3 2 1

Library and Archives Canada Cataloguing in Publication

Sebe, Masayuki, 1953–
    100 animals on parade! / written and illustrated by Masayuki Sebe.

Translation of: Dôbutsu parade 100.
ISBN 978-1-55453-871-3

1. Counting — Juvenile literature. 2. Animals — Juvenile literature.
I. Title. II. Title: One hundred animals on parade!.

QA113.S43513 2013   j513.2'11   C2012-904551-9

Kids Can Press is a ℓ◉ℾᑌS™ Entertainment company